LAWRENCE TOMS

ONLINE NETWORK MARKETING

The Ultimate Guide to Multilevel Marketing, Discover the Best Techniques and Practices on How to Build a Successful Online Network Marketing Business

Descrierea CIP a Bibliotecii Naţionale a României
LAWRENCE TOMS
 ONLINE NETWORK MARKETING. The Ultimate Guide to Multilevel Marketing, Discover then Best Techniques and Practices on How to Build a Successful Online Network **Marketing Business** / Lawrence Toms – Bucharest: Editura My Ebook, 2020
 ISBN

LAWRENCE TOMS

ONLINE NETWORK MARKETING

The Ultimate Guide to Multilevel Marketing, Discover the Best Techniques and Practices on How to Build a Successful Online Network Marketing Business

My Ebook Publishing House
Bucharest, 2020

TABLE OF CONTENTS

INTRODUCTION

What are the secrets to building an ultra-successful network marketing business? If you were to ask 30 top distributors and industry leaders, you'd get 30 different answers with many areas of commonality. Each would also possess some totally unique insights into what it takes derived from their own field experiences that would not necessarily be shared by the others.

For more than 50 years, throughout the great profession of network marketing, the gift of a life-changing income, the opportunity to take part in fun and fulfilling work, and the chance to forever impact the lives of countless others has been shared by many top leaders and expert trainers in their own ways. Each of these extraordinary individuals has been successful in conveying the essential principles that have allowed their students (downline) to go out and touch the lives of countless others, creating wealth and with it, personal freedom in the process.

All of these experts, in building their personal fortunes through the vehicle of network marketing, have developed their own insights into what this process requires. And each has acquired some very special success distinctions that have supported their teams to duplicate their achievements to some degree. That is the very special gift that network marketing embodies: Those who reach top levels of accomplishment must have done so by supporting several others to duplicate their success and build networking dynasties of their own. No other profession better rewards its members for the exact levels of success they are able to convey to others. Networkers truly earn what they are worth!

Chapter 1

Why Online MLM

MLM survival. Let's face it, the world out there is like a jungle. More particularly so in the MLM world. It would be easy to say, since it is that difficult, let's just forget about the whole MLM or network marketing deal in the first place. The basis of network marketing is building networks of people who buy and sell products. What better place to build a network of people than on the ultimate worldwide network - the internet? According to Internet World Stats, as of 2016, there were more than 1 billion people online worldwide. It's no wonder that the internet is *the* place to go to build a network marketing business.

The benefits to building your business online are extensive - you can work in shorts and a T-shirt, you only talk with people who are highly interested, your business is working for you 24/7, your maintenance costs are low, and it's easy to expand internationally. Most important, anyone can do it - you don't have to be a computer genius to find success.

Passive Income

First of all, it gives you passive income. What does passive income stand for? Passive income is an income received on a regular basis, with little effort required to maintain it. It is closely related to the concept of "unearned income". This is one of the few most viable methods to earning a residual income for effort you invest in.

Unlike other residual income vehicles like providing a service or membership sites, you don't have to have your own product!

Same Effort But Better

Secondly, network marketing takes almost the same effort as affiliate marketing only better. Contrary to popular opinion, doing online Network Marketing takes about the same effort as promoting affiliate programs. However, unlike typical affiliate programs however, you get paid over and over again! Plus, you can ride on multi-tier commissions generated from your downlines!

Beats Traditional Network Marketing

The best part about online network marketing is it beats traditional network marketing. Most conventional Network Marketing companies are marketed the traditional way which is meet prospects face to face. But, with the Internet, you can find prospect without leaving home! Just by sitting in front of your computer with a nice cup of coffee, you are earning! How awesome is that! Furthermore, it is easier to automate and scale your online network marketing business. Everything is digitalize, you can save your effort, time and money all at the same time!

Chapter 2

Nine Things For Achieving Network

Marketing Success

Capital in your network marketing business isn't what matters. It isn't the money that buys you a future; it's your skills that buy you a future. Money and no skills, I'm telling you, you are still poor. Money and no ambition, where are you? Money and no courage, you're broke. A little bit of money and a whole lot of courage is all we need. By selling and buying you are simply sharing from your own excitement and belief about the product and the opportunity. Once the customer says yes, ask for the money and then go get the product. After doing this three or four times, you will be able to buy and sell, but never let money keep you from an opportunity when you have in its place true ambition, faith, and courage.

So, let's recap and break it down a bit further. When starting any enterprise or business, whether it is full-time or part-time, we all know the value of having plenty of capital (money). But I bet we both know or at least have heard of people who started with no capital who went on to make fortunes. This is particularly true in the network marketing profession. I believe there are actually some things that are more valuable than capital that can lead to your entrepreneurial success in building a thriving network marketing business. Let me give you the list.

Time

Time is more valuable than capital. The time you set aside not to be wasted, not to be given away. Time you set aside to be invested in an enterprise that brings value to the marketplace with the hope of making a profit. Now we have capital time. How valuable is time? Time properly invested is worth a fortune. Time wasted can be devastation. Time invested can perform miracles, so you invest your time.

Desperation

I have a friend named Lydia whose first major investment in her new network marketing business was desperation. She said, "My kids are hungry, I've got to make this work. If this doesn't work, what will I do?" So she invested $1 in her enterprise selling a product she believed in. The $1 was to buy a few flyers so she could make a sale at retail, collect the money, and then buy the product wholesale to deliver back to the customer.

Determination

Determination says "I will." First Lydia said, "I must find a customer." Desperation. Second, she said, "I will find someone before this first day is over." Sure enough, she found someone. She said, "If it works once, it will work again." But then the next person said no. Now what must you invest?

Courage

Courage is more valuable than capital. If you've got only $1 and a lot of courage, I'm telling you, you've got a good future ahead of you. Courage in spite of the circumstances.

Humans can do the most incredible things no matter what happens. Haven't we heard the stories? There are some recent ones from Afghanistan and Iraq that some of the most classic, unbelievable stories of being in the depths of hell and finally making it out. You can't sell humans short. Courage in spite of, not because of, but in spite of. Now once Lydia has made three or four sales and gotten going, here's what now takes over.

Ambition

"Wow! If I can sell 3, I can sell 33. If I can sell 33, I can sell 103." Wow. Lydia is now dazzled by her own dreams of the future.

Faith

Now she begins to believe she has got a good product. This is probably a good company. And she then starts to believe in herself. Lydia, single mother, two kids, no job. "My gosh, I'm going to pull it off!" Her self-esteem starts to soar. These are investments that are unmatched. Money can't touch it. What if you had a million dollars and no faith? You'd be poor; you wouldn't be rich. Now here is the next one, the reason why she's a millionaire today.

Ingenuity

Put your brains to work. Probably up until now, you've put about one-tenth of your brainpower to work. What if you employed the other nine-tenths? You wouldn't believe what can happen. Humans can come up with the most intriguing things to do. Ingenuity. What's ingenuity worth? A fortune. It is more valuable than money. All you need is a $1 and plenty of ingenuity. Figuring out a way to make it work, make it work, make it work.

Heart and Soul

What is a substitute for heart and soul? It's not money. Money can't buy heart and soul. Heart and soul are more valuable than a million dollars. A million dollars without heart and soul, you have no life. You are ineffective. But heart and soul are like the unseen magic that moves people, moves people to buy, moves people to make decisions, moves people to act, moves people to respond.

Personality

You've just got to spruce up and sharpen up your own personality. You've got plenty of personality. Just get it developed to where it is effective every day no matter who you talk to - whether it is a child or a businessperson, whether it is a rich person or a poor person. A unique personality that is at home anywhere.

This entire list is more valuable than money. With $1 and the list I just gave you, you can harness the power inherent in the vehicle of network marketing and the world is yours. It belongs to you, whatever piece of it you desire, whatever development you wish for your life. I've given you the secret. Capital. The kind of capital that is more valuable than money and that can secure your future and fortune. Remember that you lack not the resources.

Chapter 3

How To Generate Leads

Generating leads, both high in quantity and quality is a marketer most important objective. A successful lead generation engine is what keeps the funnel full of sales prospects while you sleep. Surprisingly, only 1 in 10 marketers feel their lead generation campaigns are effective. What gives? There can be a lot of moving parts in any lead generation campaign and often times it's difficult to know which parts need fine tuning. In this video, we are going to touch on the lead generation methods.

Email Advertising

Email advertising, also known as email marketing, it is the simplest yet most effective way to generate leads. Research from Experian states that $1 invested in email marketing initiatives still yields roughly $44.25 return for marketers. This fact illuminates consumers' familiarity and comfort with email, and additionally the universality of this marketing medium. In this post I would like to uncover some of the dos and don'ts of email marketing and some best practices to utilize for generating and nurturing new leads.

Marketing automation software allows marketers to build out email marketing "tracks" from within the software. A marketing track is a collection of emails delivered over time for a specific type of buyer, or a distinct area of interest. Let me illustrate by way of example. If you were a marketing manager at an IT consulting firm you might build out marketing tracks for individuals like: the technical buyer, the financial buyer, and the end user. Additionally, you might build out marketing tracks for topics like, data security, scalable infrastructure, and system backup. As the marketer you're able to create and schedule these email in advance, allowing you to more efficiently craft cohesive communication that will be highly valuable to your audience. Then once your marketing tracks have been developed you can quickly and easily place people into these correspondence streams either manually or based on user behaviour triggers. This consistent and highly relevant email communication helps you build credibility and trust with leads.

Additionally it keep your brand top- of-mind for when decision makers are ready to select a solution.

When developing email marketing tracks geared at moving leads deeper into the sales funnel, there are a few design and copywriting elements that marketers should be mindful of. Below are a list of these tactics:

1. **Subject Line:** The subject line is how leads determine if they are going to read your email. So spend time on thinking about ways you can improve your subject line. Some ideas are: create subject lines that clearly address your leads business problems, personalize subject lines, and make subject lines actionable like: "attend our webinar" or "download our latest e-book".

2. **Brevity**: Leads and prospects are bombarded with massive amounts of email every day. So keep your email concise and engaging.

3. **Imagery**: To quote a fellow inbound marketer Amanda Sibley, the brain comprehends images 60,000 times faster than text. So by using images that reinforce your copy you more quickly deliver your message to your intended audience.

4. **Social Integration**: As marketers we want our readers to be sharing our content with their network and the best way to facilitate this is by incorporating social media sharing links into your emails. Additionally, each recipient of the email will have their own favourite social network so give them options to share on Google+, Facebook, Twitter, or Linkedin.

5. **CTA**: To effectively move leads further into the sales funnel you need educate them on your product or service. The way to educate them is to have them consume your content: whether that content be: e-books, webinars, case studies, slide-shares or videos. So in your email you need to effectively advertise your CTA. Use action words like: attend, download, register, read, and try now. Give them a next step to take after reading your email, like registering for an upcoming webinar.

Forum Prospecting

As for forums prospecting, new customers represent the life blood of a vital, growing company. As competition for new customers increases in every market and customers themselves become more savvy buyers, successful sales organizations must take their prospecting game to a higher level. Playing the so-called "numbers game" (high-volume cold-calling) is no longer enough for increasing your yield of qualified prospects in today's commercial markets. High-performing sales professionals now take a strategic approach to their prospecting activities, in order to generate a continuously flowing pipeline of qualified leads.

Strategic Prospecting helps salespeople to increase their prospecting productivity - and especially increase their ratio of initial calls to qualified-customer meetings - by focusing the salespeople on offerings that their prospects find valuable and different. The program provides a framework for operating effectively in today's hypercompetitive market, which is increasingly shaped by Web 2.0 social media tools. It also proposes a reliable prospecting method, and skills, tools, and tactics for generating and prioritizing qualified leads, engaging potential prospects, securing meetings, and handling prospects' objections. Strategic Prospecting is designed for salespeople operating in a competitive selling environment and actively developing their territory. Participants should bring a solid understanding of their organization's selling process and be able to move sales situations forward by consistently applying fundamental selling skills.

Start A Facebook Group

The biggest and most happening social media among us would definitely be Facebook. And so, generating leads with Facebook is quite an easy task as long as you know the right way to use. Start a Facebook group to for your existing Downlines and motivate them to bring their own Downlines in. You can have your group to be open so everyone will be able to see the content of your group. But, you need to know there are pros and cons about having an open Facebook group.

WhatsApp Group

Besides a Facebook group, a WhatsApp group is essential too. Of course it may not be as good as Facebook group in visual but, it is good when it comes to interaction. Having a WhatsApp group is like having a small forum on your phone. You can interact with your group member anytime anywhere as long as there is Internet connection. There is no boundary and easier excess compared to Facebook group where you used comment.

Chapter 4

The Pros And Cons

The basic structure of a network marketing business is similar to that of any established corporation, where you are your own boss and are solely responsible for your actions. These types of businesses are not only highly profitable but are also more exciting, as you will be able to reach out to an ever-increasing number of network participants coming from varied backgrounds and locations. You will not be alone in your initiatives, as all the network participants will strive together to achieve a common goal.

The Pros

In such businesses, there is no end to opportunities, as you can continue to earn profits as long as your network keeps growing. The network's growth mostly depends on personal recommendations and not on advertising or marketing. Your benefits will increase with an increase in the number of new members joining the network.

Meaning that you will have your lasting passive income compared to income generated by affiliate marketing and one-time sales. Plus, with the Internet, you can join more than one Network Marketing company and not restrict yourself to just one.

These types of businesses are preferred because they allow you to take risks without costing you thousands of dollars. You just have to try it once to find out whether it works for you or not. Even if you do not succeed, it will not affect your finances because just like the entry costs, the exit costs are also negligible. The best part of these businesses is that even after exiting the business, you will continue to receive residual income and the applicable tax benefits.

The Cons

Nothing is perfect. As for network marketing, you need to accept that you don't truly own the business. You are a distributor regardless of your level within the company.

Also, like every other business, it takes time to grow your downlines before you see geometric growth in your network and income. The start-up costs that you will be required to pay may be small, but are nevertheless necessary and you have to make it available at the time of starting the business. You need to decide well in advance the time you are willing to dedicate to your new business. These businesses are not like the typical 9 to 5 jobs and you may have to allocate a lot of time at the start for developing the desired network base. You need to conduct proper research for gathering information about available options such as the markets that can be targeted and the available networking channels. You also need to make available the necessary infrastructure such as computers and other communication devices.

For most people, online MLM has a negative connotation to it. Despite so, direct selling remains one of the fastest growing industries. Network marketing business offers unlimited profitability and job satisfaction. If you have the passion to make it to the top without taking too many risks, then network marketing is probably the best option for you. The best thing is that, it is expected to grow even more popular by the years!

Chapter 5

The Power Of A Great System

Most people fail in network marketing because they are not given a clear road map, a system, to follow. Without this type of well-defined system, many new independent representatives can quickly become discouraged. They do not experience the success that first enticed them to become involved in our industry and quickly lose passion, excitement, and commitment.

Did you know that, according to industry averages, 8 out of 10 people who sign up with a direct-sales/network marketing company stay less than one year? Most people would agree that they work too hard recruiting to experience that level of loss and frustration. An effective system can be instrumental in addressing two essential areas - first, it will help equip new enrolees to achieve quick and consistent success, and second, it sets the stage for long-term retention. As all network marketers know, the more positive and rewarding the experience, the longer people will remain active in the opportunity.

It is vital that people realize the power of following a system that includes a fast way to get started. A great example of this power is the McDonald's franchise chain.

Whether you order a Big Mac in New York, Hong Kong, or anywhere in between, you will get the very same taste, same ingredients, and same packaging. You see, Ray Kroc realized a very important principle in successful business, and that is the power of an easily and consistently followed system.

Always help people realize that they are starting an actual business. Help them understand that they are not just buying product; they are the CEO of their own national or worldwide business. Build up the integrity of the business they are involved in as well as the network marketing industry, and the vast potential of both their business and this industry. The network marketing industry has created more millionaires than any other industry, including real estate, and has attained a high level of respect as a very viable and legitimate industry. Additionally, this exciting industry offers individuals an opportunity to create very formidable businesses with incomes rivaling or exceeding those of highly paid executives. There are four initial activities you want a new enrolee to do, and these should be accomplished either with the help of the person who brought the enrolee into the business or by a qualified team leader.

Establish Goals

The first thing a new enrolee should do is establish goals - the "why" for building his or her network marketing business. This is an exciting time as people are encouraged to take all the limitations off of their circumstances and to actually begin to consider their real potential. Many times, the process of setting goals and attaching them to dreams and desires can be absolutely explosive. There is a great deal of emotion connected to setting goals, because we all have dreams of glorious accomplishments and we all want to create an impressive legacy. These goals cannot be about just money, although money usually funds a goal. The goal must be a tangible, material accomplishment, such as college funding for a child, support for a ministry or charity, a new home, or the financial freedom of being debt free. The more emotion that is attached to a goal, the stronger the drive is within an individual to accomplish that goal. You become unswervingly committed to achieving the goal.

This is also the time when a new enrolee should be encouraged to plug into the company's recognition program. Many times, specific actions tied to a recognition program actually fuel team growth and increased income. As new enrolees begin to build their businesses by following a proven system, they also begin to realize success in achieving daily goals. These daily goals build into life-changing goals, and soon what was only a dream becomes a reality. Many top producers will confirm that as team members earn recognition awards, excitement and momentum will build within an organization. This type of momentum causes a business to experience explosive growth and success.

Make A Commitment

The next activity important in a new enrolee's success is to make a commitment to the business. What amount of time, resources, and effort is the person willing to devote to developing the new business? Is this level of commitment sufficient to help these goals become a reality? The level of commitment must match the size of the goals, or the goals must be adjusted to the level of commitment your new enrolee is willing to make.

Remember, honesty is crucial. Be honest with your new enrolee so his or her goals are realistic. For example, you must be sure he understands that he cannot just work his new business four hours a week and expect to make $10,000 in a short period of time. The familiar saying that you can work a network marketing business part-time but not in your spare time is very true. Today, it seems that no one has spare time.

So treat your business as a business, not an occasional diversion, and encourage your team members to have that same mind-set. It is only logical to realize that in order to generate income and business-building activity, one must commit to talking to a certain number of people each day, each week, each month. Set aside specific hours each week for your new business, and commit to work your business during those hours. Do not give in to excuses or procrastination.

It is essential that people commit to educating themselves about the incredible business we are in. Network marketing, or direct sales, truly offers the kind of independence and prosperity that our country's founders envisioned and longed for. This industry is one of the few areas where a level playing field is available to anyone, regardless of age, gender, education, or social station.

Develop A Prospect List

Now we are up to the third activity on our list of the four things a new enrolee should do for fast success. It is important for new team members to immediately make a list of as many people as possible to whom they can present their business. This list may include 100 to 200 names, and it should always be a work in progress. Always add to your prospect list. As your new business is developed, you will continually meet new people and come in contact with prior acquaintances. Add these contacts to your prospect list and follow up with them.

One common downfall for many people as they develop prospect lists is that they first identify the poorest, most down-and-out people they can think of. They instead should be looking for the busiest, most industrious people they know! These are the people to partner with in this business. The beauty of network marketing is that you can choose with whom you work, unlike a traditional job where you simply do not have that luxury.

Other important qualities to look for when developing a prospect list are a positive, upbeat personality and the desire for more from life - more money, more time and more freedom.

These are personality traits that attract people and that cause people to look beyond their current limitations into the big, bright world of possibility.

Get Busy

Finally, I cannot stress enough just how important it is to get new team members actively approaching the people on their prospect list - again, looking for busy people, positive people, people who are hungry for more out of life. Identifying five or six people who would be the very best candidates and approaching them first can be a great way to get someone off to a fast start.

It is so important for a new person to understand that in approaching people, the initial goal is only to connect a prospect with a team leader so the leader can make the presentation. A problem that has torpedoed many new network marketing business owners is that, because they are so very excited, they go out and immediately begin talking to people, giving incorrect information or, even worse, too much information. The ensuing rejection is usually inevitable.

So how should you approach people? The purpose of approaching people is to uncover the needs in their lives that your opportunity can fill. A technique that has been used with great success by many people in the network marketing industry is the FORM method (family, occupation, recreation, and message). Now, the only way this method works is if the individual employing it disciplines himself to always keep the conversation on the prospect. Keep the main focus of the conversation on the prospect. The FORM method asks questions about the prospect's family, occupation, and favourite recreation. As the conversation unfolds, you will uncover needs in the prospect's life, whether it is a working mother who yearns to be home with her children but needs an income or a highly paid executive who has sold all his time to earn the kind of income that his career provides. Once you uncover the need, you are able to connect that need to the message of your opportunity.

Chapter 6

Stages To Achieve Freedom Well

Earned

People of diverse backgrounds find new opportunity in network marketing every day. I know a woman who owned a residential cleaning business who now makes millions from her network marketing business. I know a CEO of a $300 million company who replaced his seven-figure income and found new opportunity and freedom through his networking business. I have seen people from all backgrounds - teachers, lawyers, medical doctors, realtors, hotel bellmen, blue-collar workers, and men and women from all levels of the corporate world - find freedom through network marketing. All have a personal story about their success that is both instructive and inspiring. Each of them faced unique personal challenges and obstacles while building their businesses. Overcoming these personal challenges is the price you pay for your freedom. Each of them now enjoys a great lifestyle and uncommon success, filled with personal satisfaction and freedom. Each of them earned their freedom and lifestyle through hard work, commitment, focus, and persistence.

It doesn't matter what you have or haven't accomplished in the past, how long your resume is, what education credentials you have or don't have; it is about knowledge and action. Freedom is about choice and a decision to act. Your commitment to take action and learn from your results and consistently pursue your goals will determine your level of success. I believe everyone can commit to an action plan and achieve a new level of personal success. The freedom achieved through network marketing is unparalleled.

Stage 1: *Getting Started*

Getting started is the most difficult part of any new venture. Adding something new to an already busy life and career can seem impossible at times. Stage one will demand more from you than you would give to a regular job. But it is your business, and the rewards are worth the effort. It's like learning to play chess. You have to learn the basics first. Each piece on the board does something completely different, and you need to learn how to deploy them effectively. Knowing how the pieces move is not enough; you also have to respond to your opponent's moves. As you progress, you begin to learn different strategies to respond to each situation. It takes time, a willingness to learn, and patience.

Action

Developing an action plan for your business is the first step toward success. Write down all the reasons and motivations that describe why you chose to start a business. Your well-thought-through reasons will become the driving force behind your success. Define your purpose for being in business and a vision of where you're going. Set goals for immediate action. Set a specific schedule of your work hours. It is easier to get off to a fast start and build consistently than it is to start slowly with an inconsistent effort. Consistency is a behaviour or a principle of success that is critical to a good start. Following your action plan and holding yourself accountable to specific measurable results each day, week, and month will ensure that you make progress toward your goals. In this stage clarity, commitment, consistency, and action are four principles of success that determine how fast you reach your goals.

Prospecting

Our primary job as networkers is to help people to help themselves to a better life. We help people build a better life through the use of our products and services and economically through their involvement in our business model. Your success as a team builder is secured by developing the business skills and the personal skills required to attract, enrol, train, and develop the talents of others. Prospecting is the art of finding others who also have the desire to build a business of their own.

Therefore, as networkers, we must stay focused on this objective. We can only help people reach the goals they are willing to set for themselves. We can't make people successful. To truly help others in this business, our prospects must want something new or be open to positive change in their lives. Our prospects must realize that their current circumstances need to change, and that to live the life they aspire to they need to change, develop, and grow as individuals. And finally, they come to understand that our business model can deliver exactly what they want and more.

That understanding fuels their commitment to change and grow. Without that commitment to change and grow, they are not prospects, just suspects. Learning this lesson will help you to stay focused on working with the right people and to invest your time wisely. Talk with a number of people in order to get practice. I teach dozens of different prospecting techniques, so that anyone can find three to five techniques that will work best for them.

Feel Like Quitting?

In stage one you will need to monitor your expectations. As you build your business you will be in contact with many diverse people. Some will have real interest and some will seem interested but are just being polite. You will have expectations about their interest and potential contribution to your business. Disappointments come when we assume others are more interested then they actually are. Qualifying real interest will help you keep your expectations in check. As previously stated, you can only help people to help themselves to a better life. In stage one, feeling like quitting is an acceptable human emotion. However, actually quitting is unacceptable. Make a commitment that is longer than the time it takes to develop proficiency - your learning curve. That way you set yourself up for real success rather than disappointment.

Stage 2: *A Full Time Business Of Your Own*

In this phase of your development, you have learned the basics of a successful and profitable network marketing business. You are ready to take your businesses to the next level. Armed with your proven skills and new work schedule, you will find it easier to recruit people with greater capacity and skill. At this stage, you understand how to play the game and have mastered the basic strategies. You are beginning to see several moves ahead and are not surprised by your opponent's moves. On a good day, you play brilliantly.

The Challenge Of Self-Employment

When you start your networking business, you become the CEO, with the responsibilities of charting the course for the future of your business. You also become the management team responsible for the implementation of that vision. You also become the head of the human resources department responsible for recruiting and training the talent required to accomplish the objectives of the management team. You also take on the responsibilities of the head of marketing and promotion, and customer service. Juggling all these responsibilities will challenge you to step outside your comfort zone and learn new skills.

To develop a big networking business requires clear strategic thinking and a commitment to developing the right human resources to reach your goals. Stay in the building mode with a focus on recruiting stronger and more developed talent. Learn the discipline of being self-employed, and stay focused on your goals and objectives. This is an interesting challenge. You will now have much more free time to manage or mismanage. You can go golfing or stay home on a beautiful day and make the calls to new prospects. Hmm! The choice is now yours. There is no longer a boss checking up on you to see if you are getting things done. This is a new opportunity to discover your own undeveloped talents and can be one of the most rewarding and freeing personal experiences you may ever have.

Personal Development

Personal development is the process of developing more of what you have as latent potential within. Reaching your full potential as a human being consists of two different processes.

One is the process of acquiring new characteristics and attributes such as patience, courage, determination, self-confidence, and trustworthiness. The second process is correcting old habits, the wearing away of the rough edges of your personality, like shyness, fearfulness, or unworthiness. This is the process where we lose or release the behaviours that no longer work for us.

Stepping outside your comfort zone is an act of courage. It's also where the excitement is and where real personal growth begins.

An analogy that best illustrates this point is to look at our behaviour like driving a car. We control the steering, transmission, brake, and the accelerator. The steering keeps us moving in the direction we want to go. The transmission is our human potential and current skills. The accelerator is our focus, excitement, and confidence that power us forward. The brakes are our fears that stop us or hold us back. When used appropriately, they provide for safe mobility. However, when we step outside our comfort zone, we respond to our fears and or excitement by putting our foot on the brake or on the accelerator and sometimes both. How we use these controls determines how fast we grow and reach more of our potential.

Stage 3: *Privileged Lifestyle – Freedom*

This stage is the culmination of all your plans and efforts. You have worked hard and learned much. You have well-developed skills and proven command of the business. You think and act on long-term goals and objectives. You are free! You have developed a group of strong full-time leaders. They are trained and growing without your involvement. They look to you for guidance and support on the bigger issues of planning and leadership development. You have the respect of your peers and the admiration of your corporate leaders. You are now the chess master. You see the outcome of the game before you move your first piece. You know all the gambits; you know where your opponent is going before he or she makes the next move. Each move you make flows seamlessly into the next. You are rarely surprised; you are in control of the board.

Leadership

Most of the leaders I have met in network marketing have worked hard on both themselves and their businesses. Many are articulate, have a great sense of humour, are great storytellers, have great product knowledge, have a deep understanding of the fundamentals of network marketing, and have high energy, natural excitement, and have a well-developed self-image and confidence. They inspire the best in the people around them. By working on yourself as much as on the business, you can develop your own style of leadership.

At this stage, your consistent efforts have paid off. You love this game, both for what it has given you and for what it has allowed you to give others. You have earned the right to true freedom! Your experiences have made you a better person and a better leader. You have met your own personal challenges and those victories have fuelled your confidence and personal success. It is never easy, but you did it! Freedom at this level is its own reward. When others say you are lucky to have such success and freedom, you'll know with certainty that the freedom you have is a freedom well earned.

Chapter 7

How To Scale Your Online Network

Marketing

For many people the subject of recruiting is the deathblow to their network marketing dreams.

Does it have to be this way? Why do so many people join multi-level marketing organizations, only to dropout in disgust within the month? There is no denying this fact: Recruiting can be tough. The toughest thing about recruiting is not approaching people and discussing the opportunity, your enthusiasm for the business will see you through any hesitancy in this area. Lack of interest and outright refusal on the part of your prospects, however, can demoralize you.

Disappointment and discouragement can eat through your excitement for this business like rust through the hull of an aircraft carrier - and that's what sinks the bulk of us. Not rust, discouragement. How do you keep from becoming discouraged?

It's easy for people to say, "Keep your chin up," or "Keep trying, a positive attitude will see you through." But verbal encouragement can only get you so far.

Tips To Grow Your Downlines

In order to grow your downlines or in other word, recruiting, you may offer your support to them. Help your downlines that are more pro-active to close sale on their behalf whenever they bring in prospect. Once your downline inspire a prospect to join your organization, you need to support him until he gains his "network marketing legs." You may even allow your downlines to duplicate your online system and train them to generate leads like you are doing.

A new prospect needs to be encouraged, even baby-sit to a certain degree. Most importantly, a new associate needs to be appreciated. Let her know that she is a part of the team, and that her individual development and success is both wanted and critical to the success of the organization. Reward her frequently with t-shirts or other inexpensive gifts for achieving predetermined levels of growth and sales volume, and of course, help her establish new goals and action plans.

Have you ever walked into a new job and not been given the benefit of a trainer?

What does it feel like when a boss tells you to get the job done, but doesn't offer to tell you how to do it? That's how the new recruit feels when you sign him up and say, "Go to it, buddy. You can do it." This is not enough. Not everyone will share your enthusiasm let alone succeed in this business. You need to train them to become one. But it's always the 5% to 10% of the serious action takers that will actively promote the online network marketing opportunity.

Chapter 8

How To Promote Online MLM

As you know, promoting a business has its own technique to be used. Not every business shared the same promoting technique. And so, it is important for you to understand your business style and also your target audiences.

Follow Up Series

From day one in your online MLM business, you should start building a list. The money is in the list! I am talking about building an email list of people who give you permission to contact them. You need start collecting names and emails in your auto responder, right from the day you started. The sooner you start building a list the better off you will be.

An auto-responder is simply a software program that lets you automatically create, edit and manage an email list. Once you have your capture page setup for your business, you need to sign up for an auto-responder service so you can start building a list. In this case, I would strongly recommend Aweber. Why? This is because they are reasonably priced and have high deliverability rates. Once you sign up for the auto responder service, you will copy and paste a code from your auto responder onto your capture page. This creates a form where people can type in their name and email and automatically be added to your list.

In additions, you can schedule your emails. Once someone signs up for your list, they will automatically start getting your emails at the frequency you choose. You can choose whatever frequency you want. But, not spamming. Spamming will only annoyed your subscribers and drift them away from you. I suggest you send at least two emails per week. That way you keep in touch with your prospect on a regular basis, so they won't forget about you and yet, they are not annoyed.

Creating A Website

Most of the people do not have the idea of creating their own website to promote their business. But, I have to tell you this, if you spend some time getting the idea of creating a website and doing some SEO, you can actually get high quality leads from all over the world. Millions of people all over the world search Google for checking the reviews and other details. You need to optimize your website in such a way that your website appears on the first page of Google for many of such keywords. And of course, you need to include your company details in your website so that people will visit your website, read about your company and if they are interested, they will contact you for further details.

Another important thing is your landing page of your website. A good landing page will attract more interests in people. When it comes to building your online MLM business, everything starts with a landing page. A landing page is a one page website that is designed to capture a prospect's attention and entice them to give your their name and email. A good landing page has a headline, a few key benefits, a call to action and sometimes a video. You should not use more than 120 words on a page and you should not have other links on the page.

Through Forums And Comments On MLM Topics

Another best way to promote your business will be through comments and forums on online MLM topics. You need to find blogs who has written articles on online network marketing. You need to leave a good comment along with your company details ad contact number so that others can see this and contact you. Many people try to promote their MLM companies through the comment section. So in this way, you can search Google with different keywords on online network marketing and leave your comment on the site you find through search.

Another way to promoting online is through online network marketing forums. There are hundreds of high traffic forums on network marketing. You can search Google with keywords like online network marketing. You can join these forums and contribute in questions and answer. You can promote your business either through signature link or in the question-answers.

Through Facebook Pages

Also, you can create a Facebook page with the name of your company. And then you will need to promote your

Facebook page so that people "Like" your page, become the fan and in future, your customer. You should use a professional profile photo and profile description in your page. Using a proper profile photo is very important in convincing people. Design a legit looking graphic for your company, it will make a huge different. Trust me.

Also, you can use paid feature of Facebook advertising to boost your post. You can get thousands of potential fans in just few dollars. Remember, more Facebook fans means more conversion. Besides, you should start commenting with your company account and be active in any related groups or pages. Leaving your company details in the comment doesn't harm. In fact, people who are interested in your company will eventually come to you. But of course, you need to be helpful in commenting in the first place. If you are able to give proper answer to resolve a problem, you are earning people's trust in conjunctionally.

Chapter 9

Which Online Networking Marketing

Company to Join

No man is an island in this world. Up-lines will always be there to help but the attitude to be adopted is that I am in business for myself but not by myself. Since I am in business for myself, I am the master of my fate, I create my own luck, and I am the author of my own book – it all boils down to ME. Having an up-line to help you is considered a BONUS. If you were to run a traditional business, would you expect other people to open shop for you and close the shop for you? Same goes in MLM.

Basic Guidelines

No one has succeeded in any industry without learning and MLM is no different. It is the up-line's responsibility to guide, train, teach and motivate the downline. New people in MLM without guidance are like sheep wandering into a wild forest – what are their chances of survival? It is no wonder 95% of Network Marketers fail to break even. The up-line must lead them, empower them but must never spoon feed them. Up-lines must not be abused. If you give a man a fish, he will feed himself for a day. Teach him to fish, and he will feed himself for life! I won't recommend any network marketing company in particular, but, I am here to offer some guidelines and a check list for you to consider before committing yourself to any online Network Marketing company.

The management team is the backbone of your business. They are your suppliers and your collection agents all in one. How can you survive in the network marketing industry if your suppliers are not delivering the goods on time or the company has cash flow problems?

In order to choose the right company with the right management team, you must do your due diligence on these factors:

Their track record. Is the network marketing company backed by a solid track record?

Is the team here to stay? There are some network company owners who build and burn and build again. You don't want to invested interest in a company that is there today but gone tomorrow!

The vision. Does the company have a solid vision and are they actively working towards that vision?

The capacity to expand. Sometimes, when a new start-up company is expanding, they might run into cash flow problems when their sales volume increase! They need to build more warehouse, deal with shipment and pay more commissions and bank loans when more and more orders are taken. Just because the teams are growing and the sales are coming in doesn't mean the company is able to cope.

Types Of Compensation Plans

The plan is very important. It shows how much work you need to do to get paid this much. All marketing plans have their own advantages and disadvantages. Different companies offer different margins for their products. The key to remember in margin comparison, if the company pays the distributor too low, you might not survive; if the margin is too exorbitantly high, you might earn a lot, but your retail customers will suffer and the business might not be long term.

There are many types of compensation plans out there. Some of them are so complex that it requires a degree in mathematics to figure out how much money you will get in your next commission check! Some people tend to neglect compensation plans. They feel that it is not important at the initial stages. But if you are not very clear how to „place" your downlines, you will LOSE A LOT OF INCOME and in some cases, some of your downlines will lose vested interest if you fail to place the right people under them. Remember, losing 10% may not seem like a big amount but when you calculate in the long run, your sales volume could total up to THE THOUSANDS and it is even worse when it is not YOUR income because if you cause your downline to lose money due to poor planning then you will lose the trust in your leadership which is something money can't buy back!

Uni-level

Uni-level plans are one of the oldest compensation plan structures in the world and their calculation is very straight forward. Basically you are able to sponsor as many people as you can and you can draw commissions up to a certain level. In other words – unlimited width, limited depth. A person in a Uni-level plan should focus on building as many team leaders as possible. Sponsor up to 4 to 5 people and focus on helping them build their groups (rather than building FOR them). After all, there are only 5 days in a week, helping one at a time is enough to keep one's hands full. Don't build too wide to the point that you can't help your people and they are left all alone.

Breakaway

The concept of breakaway or in other words stair steps plan is similar to the Uni-level structure but the payment and building structure is a bit different. Basically you focus building your „rank" by climbing the Stairstep ladder of success. You usually achieve this creating or helping your downline to create sales volume. Once you achieve a certain rank, you can override commissions up to infinity levels. Just like the Uni-level plan, you must focus on creating leaders in your FRONTLINE – those that you directly sponsor. Because it is worthless to have a large width of frontline when they are not producing anything.

Matrix

Matrix plans are often even more complex than the other plans above but basically you will need to fill a number of

UNITS in a matrix cycle (consisting of a fixed width and depth – in the case above, it is a 2 by 2 matrix). When a matrix is "filled", you will be given a new account that you can use to build a new matrix and earn more money.

Binary

Binary plans and building structures are usually more complex because you are only allowed to have a width of 2 and place the people you sponsor under your downlines.

In other words – 2 width, unlimited depth. In a binary plan, you often have to balance both sides of your groups by ensuring that the volume produced on the left group is almost the same as the right group. Placements of downline must always work towards balancing and you have to think not only about yourself, but for your downline as well.

9 786069 837177

Printed by Libri Plureos GmbH in Hamburg, Germany